Enchanted Evenings

323 Nights Out to Remember

Gregory J.P. Godek

CASABLANCA PRESS®
A DIVISION OF SOURCEBOOKS, INC.®
NAPERVILLE, ILLINOIS

Published by Sourcebooks, Inc.
P.O. Box 4410, Naperville, Illinois 60567-4410
(630) 961-3900
FAX: (630) 961-2168

Library of Congress Cataloging-in-Publication Data

Godek, Gregory J.P., 1955-
        Enchanted Evenings: 323 nights out to remember / Gregory Godek.
        p. cm.
        ISBN 1-57071-728-1 (alk. paper)
        1. Dating (Social customs)—Miscellanea. I. Title.

HQ801 .G5544 2001
636.7'7—dc21
                                                                                00-052654

Printed and bound in the United States of America.
PX 10 9 8 7 6 5 4 3 2 1

Dedication

To those who see dating as a way of relating,
and not merely impressing.
And, of course, to my Bride—my date, my mate.

Contents

Introduction

$\mathscr{D}$ating should be taught in school, don't you think? Not only are dating skills more important than algebra, they will serve you throughout your life l-o-o-o-n-g after quadratic equations cease having the slightest relevance to your existence.

But since dating isn't taught in school, we'll just have to teach ourselves, won't we? In my seventeen years of presenting Romance Classes, researching love, and interviewing couples, I've learned that love must be lived and expressed if it is to stay alive. I've also learned that dating is one of the best—and simplest—ways of keeping love alive.

Whether you're single or married, successful dating is about expressing love, expressing yourself, and getting to know your partner. It's about doing things together, creating shared memories, and acknowledging one another. This book is a collection of old and new ideas—from the *1001 Ways to Be Romantic* series of books, from my seminars, and from my readers—all designed to turn you into a dating dynamo.

My hope is that you become inspired to keep dating throughout your life, and that you become the inspiration for younger couples looking for romantic role models.

Gregory J.P. Godek

Romantic Days

1

One day in the Romance Class, Nancy G. told us that she and her husband have instituted a "Play Day" once a month. The class quickly leaped on the idea and expanded upon it. So, we now have couples celebrating their own "Music Days," "Food Days," and—of course—"Sex Days."

2

You could create special "themes" for various days.

- A "food" theme: Focus your entire day around food. Prepare a special breakfast. Go shopping at a farmers' market. Plan many tasty surprises for your partner throughout the day.

- A "sensual" theme: Focus your entire day around your five senses. Create experiences that heighten your appreciation of the sensual aspects of life. Give each other body massages. Watch the sunrise. Bake bread so you can appreciate the aroma. Attend a concert to appreciate the sounds.

↝ A "sexual" theme: Focus your entire day around the expression and celebration of your sexual natures. Touch each other often, from the moment you wake up in the morning. Dress provocatively. Make love several times, in several locations, throughout the day. Rent some erotic movies. Act out a favorite fantasy.

3

*W*eekdays are for working, and weekends are for relaxing. Says who?! Even though Saturday and Sunday are great days for romance, so are Monday, Tuesday, Wednesday, Thursday, and Friday! While "Weekend Romance" can be leisurely and event-filled, "Weekday Romance" can be spontaneous, quick, and fun! Think about it.

Romantic Nights

4

Dinner by candlelight. The classics always work (as long as you get the kids out of the picture and unplug the phone).

5

On your way home from work, pick up a bottle of champagne and one red rose.

6

Take all the furniture out of your dining room. Roll up the rug. Move your stereo speakers into the room. Dig out your favorite dance tunes. Greet him or her at the door dressed in your finest…and dance the night away!

Cheap Dates

7

*N*ote: There's a significant difference between being a cheap date and going on a cheap date!

8

*M*ovie matinees. Cheap but still fun.

9

*G*o shopping at secondhand shops and vintage clothing stores. It might spark some fun dress-up fantasies!

10

*Y*our basic wine and cheese picnic.

Inspired Dates

11

What's more inspiring than a magnificent sunrise—or a spectacular sunset? Pack a breakfast, head for a quiet spot, and enjoy the sunrise together. Or make time for a sunset dinner.

12

Take a seminar together: a Dale Carnegie class or Tony Robbins seminar will inspire you and help your relationship in many ways!

13

Grab some crayons or markers, title two sheets of poster paper "100 Reasons Why I Love You," and spend an evening (or two) expressing your appreciation for your mate.

Classic Dates

14

*D*inner and a movie. Note: see the movie first. That way you won't have to rush through dinner. Plus, you can discuss the movie afterward over a leisurely meal.

15

*D*inner and dancing. (And if you don't know how to dance, sign up for some dance classes! Between the lessons and your own practice sessions, you'll be busy for months!)

16

A bicycle built for two.

17

A walk on the beach.

18

A stroll in the park.

19

The scene: a pond. The equipment: a canoe. The food: picnic style. The characters: the two of you.

Classy Dates

20

Hire a pianist to come to your home and provide live background music to a private romantic dinner.

21

Hire a limousine for the evening. Dress up and go out. But don't stop anywhere—just drive around for a few hours sipping champagne and seeing the sights.

22

Take a wine tasting course together. Then attend wine tastings at various wine shops around town. This little hobby will keep you occupied and fascinated for years to come.

23

Tour a winery. Tour wineries in all forty-nine states that produce wine!

Strategies for Creating Romantic Dates

24

You say you just don't have time for romantic dates? The No.1 time-stealer is television. Try this experiment: stop watching TV for one solid month. I'll bet your time shortage will evaporate.

25

Right-brained vs. left-brained romance. Which is your style?

Right-brainers are emotional, creative, and intuitive. Left-brainers are logical, detail-oriented, and organized.

- Right-brainers tend to be good at creating experiences, moods, and memories. They'll head for a movie on a whim; cook a romantic meal from leftovers; write three love notes while their partner is looking the other way.
- Left-brainers tend to be good at planning, scheduling, and organizing. They'll create great surprise parties; never forget an anniversary; buy gifts ahead of time.

Personal Holidays

26

Let's face it: Valentine's Day puts too much pressure on all of us. This one day is going to make up for all the other days we act like romantic blockheads?! I think not. The solution? Create your own romantic holidays!

ॐCelebrate Valentine's Day on the 14th day of every month, all year round!

ॐCreate your own "Lovers' Day" in April, July, and November.

ॐCreate a floating holiday: set aside one Friday every other month; take the day off work and create a three-day escape weekend.

27

*H*ow about creating special "Half-Day Holidays"—for those of you who would have a hard time taking off a whole day of work?

Making Beautiful Music Together

28

Create a Valentine's Day concert, just for the two of you. Record an hour's worth of your favorite romantic music. Print up a program. List the song titles, along with some personal commentary about the significance of each song to you, or why particular songs remind you of her or him. Send an invitation to the concert. Dress for the event. Serve wine and cheese.

29

Romantic favorites in the Godek Music Library:

- *Shepherd Moons*, by Enya
- *In the Garden*, by Eric Tingstad & Nancy Rumbel
- *Reference Point*, by Acoustic Alchemy

30

*L*earn to sing your favorite love song together—in harmony!

31

*L*earn to sing a romantic duet! Some suggestions:

- "Almost Paradise," by Reno & Wilson
- "Nothing's Gonna Stop Us Now," by Starship
- "Always," by Atlantic Starr
- "Islands in the Stream," by Parton & Rogers
- "Somewhere Out There," by Ronstadt & Ingram
- "Time of My Life," by Medley & Warnes

32

*T*ake each other somewhere special:

- ↝ Has she seen all of her favorite singers in concert?
- ↝ Has he heard all of his favorite symphonies played live?
- ↝ Has she traveled to her dream vacation spot?
- ↝ Has he seen his favorite team play live?

Romantic Travel

33

A vacation is just a vacation—but you can turn it into a honeymoon by adding romantic elements. *Honeymoon Magazine* combines those elements. NOT for newlyweds only!

34

*S*ome travel newsletters:

- ✂ Romantic Traveling—415-731-8239

- ✂ Travel Smart—800-FARE-OFF

- ✂ Gardens & Countrysides: A Journal of Picturesque Travels—512-826-5222

- ✂ The Educated Traveler—800-648-5168

35

*W*hile on vacation, some couples spend as little as possible on accommodations and as much as possible on dining out!

Other couples pamper themselves with the most luxurious room they can find and cut corners on meals.

Some couples cut back on room and board so they can spend their money on mementos of their travels.

Travel Tips

36

Does she love ice cream as much as she loves you? Take her on a tour of Ben & Jerry's factory in Waterbury, Vermont! Call 802-882-1260.

37

Does he crave beer as much as he craves you? Take him to the world's largest brewery, Anheuser-Busch, in St. Louis, Missouri. Call 314-577-2626.

38

Is she a certified chocoholic? Take her to Hershey's Chocolate World, in Hershey, Pennsylvania. Call 717-534-4900.

A Week of Romance

39

Sunday—Read the Sunday newspapers in bed. Or go out for Sunday brunch.

40

Monday—You could make Mondays much more manageable if you get up an hour early, serve breakfast in bed, and enjoy one another's company—before facing the world.

41

Tuesday—Get the Moody Blues' CD *Days of Future Passed.* Play the song "Tuesday Afternoon." Then, schedule a little afternoon delight with your honey.

42

Wednesday—Commonly known as "Hump Day" because it's in the middle of the week…could be interpreted in another fashion, too!

43

Thursday—Pick up some videos for the weekend—beat the weekend crowds.

44

Friday—TGIF! Call in sick to work.

45

Saturday—Sleep in late. Weekend getaways. "Saturday Night at the Movies."

Good Times

46
A day at the beach.
A night at the opera.

47
A walk in the park.
A stroll down memory lane.

48
A midnight snack.
An afternoon tea.

49

A drive in the country.

A tour of the city.

Movie Dates

50

*F*avorite romantic movies (contemporary):

- When Harry Met Sally
- Bull Durham
- Flashdance
- Ghost
- Gone with the Wind

↬ A Place in the Sun

↬ Suddenly Last Summer

↬ Raintree County

↬ Splendor in the Grass

↬ Brief Encounter

↬ Frankie and Johnny

51

Favorite romantic movies (classic):

↬ A Woman of Affairs

↬ Hold Your Man

↬ Saratoga

↬ Blossoms in the Dust

↬ Maytime

- ✍ *Strike Up the Band*
- ✍ *Double Wedding*
- ✍ *Top Hat*
- ✍ *Carefree*
- ✍ *From the Terrace*
- ✍ *The Big Sleep*
- ✍ *Key Largo*

52

Create a "movie weekend" based on a theme:

- ✍ All adventure movies, romantic movies, or science fiction movies
- ✍ Movies starring her favorite actor
- ✍ Movies starring his favorite actress
- ✍ All Academy Award winning movies

෫ Foreign films

෫ All movies by a favorite writer or director

Fantasy Dates

53

"*Donald Trump Day*": Pretend you're millionaires. Test-drive a Porsche. Window-shop at Tiffany's. Try on fur coats. Visit mansions for sale.

54

"*Bonnie and Clyde Day*": Be wild! I don't recommend that you actually rob a bank—but you could certainly withdraw money from an ATM machine and pretend!

55

"Peter Pan Day": Refuse to grow up! Play hookey from work. Go to a carnival. Be silly. Buy a balloon. Play a board game.

Erotica

56

If your life was a movie…and you were going to film a scene in which you seduce your partner… and you want this scene to be elegant and romantic… how would you create this scene? What would the dialogue be? What gifts/props would you use? What would the lighting be?

57

S.O.S.—"Sex On Saturday!" Leave this "distress" message on her answering machine; mark it in his calendar; mail her S.O.S. notes; create a banner; make a "doorknob sign."

58

Some books on erotica and sex—sure to inspire some sexy dates:

- *Women Who Love Sex*, by Gina Ogden
- *203 Ways to Drive a Man Wild in Bed*, by Olivia St. Claire

Romantic Planning

59

A romantic's planning calendar:

January: Sit with your partner and review the upcoming year. Make reservations at a bed and breakfast for Valentine's Day.

February: Plan your summer vacation and any other major vacations. Plan a "Springtime Getaway" as a surprise.

March: Begin your Christmas shopping.

April: Call local theatres, symphonies, and ticket agencies to get their upcoming schedules. Order tickets well in advance.

May: Make your plans for summer.

June: Schedule a three-day escape for sometime between Memorial Day and Labor Day.

August: Plan a leaf-peeping excursion.

October: Plan a ski weekend for the upcoming winter.

November: Buy greeting cards for every occasion you can think of. Spend at least $200.

December: Look at a calendar for next year. Brainstorm twelve new romantic ideas.

A Year of Romance

60

For each month of the year, define a "theme" or "topic" to focus on as a couple. For example:

January: Renewal
February: Playing
March: Sensuality
April: Communication
May: Learning
June: Intimacy
July: Commitment
August: Celebrating
September: Self-esteem

October: Change

November: Forgiveness

December: Appreciation

61

Spin off ideas from the idea above:

- Define themes for each day of the week. You'll cycle through the list fifty-two times in a year, giving you variety and repetition.

- Define themes for your weekends.

- One couple in the Romance Class is compiling a list of 365 themes, one for each day of the year. (Some romantics are obsessed!)

Romantic Rituals

62

*D*eclare your anniversary and both of your birthdays to be your own, special "Couple's Holidays." Take those days off work and get away by yourselves. Don't let jobs or kids get in your way!

63

*W*hen you celebrate the "official" holidays of our culture, focus on the true and original meanings of the events, and don't let society's commercialism ruin it for you.

64

*C*reate your own special "holidays." I know people who celebrate the first day of summer, autumn, winter, and spring. Others celebrate the first day of school by staying home and making love in the family room! Some people celebrate the first snow fall of the year, or the first day of fishing season.

65

Create your own unique rituals. (A ritual is a special activity you perform that highlights an occasion and gives it deeper meaning.) The occasion can be commonplace or rare.

Commonplace rituals could be:

↦ Always greeting one another with a slow kiss.

↦ Preparing for lovemaking in a special, meaningful manner.

↦ A call from work at the same time every day.

Rare rituals could be:

↦ A secret toast to one another while out to dinner with friends.

↦ A unique celebration of each other's career milestones.

↦ Time spent together before one of you leaves for a trip.

66

On August 3, 1964, during a walk on the beach with his wife, Howard W. drew a heart in the sand and inscribed his initials entwined with his wife's initials. The next day when they returned to the same spot (near their home on Cape Cod, Massachusetts), the surf had washed his handiwork away. Undaunted, he drew the same message again, saying, "Love needs to be renewed every day, too." Howard has drawn the same heart and initials in the sand every day for over thirty years!

Honeymoon Heaven

67

A plain old vacation is not the same thing as a "second honeymoon!" There's a special feeling of magic and romance around a second honeymoon.

How do you create one? You start planning about a year in advance (so the anticipation builds). You buy her a stack of bridal magazines (that's where all the honeymoon destination ads are). Send travel brochures to her in the mail (with your personal notes and comments written inside). You buy special clothes.

If you do this right, it'll really spice up your life—for a year or more!

68

Go on a last-minute vacation. Don't even pack any clothes—buy them there!

69

Do you and your partner have the same "Vacation Style"? Are you an "Adventurer," "Sight-Seer," "Romantic," "Shopper," "Athlete," or "Indulger"? Do you choose vacation destinations and activities that match your styles? How do you compromise when you have different styles?

A Night on the Town

70

For some people, an evening out is about ambiance and relaxing. Dinner at a quiet, dim restaurant. Conversation at a scenic location. Taking in a local amateur theatre show.

71

For other people, an evening out is about adventure and excitement. Making the scene at the hottest nightclub. Dancing the night away. Visiting a new restaurant.

72

Have you ever tried "Restaurant-Hopping"? You spend the entire evening hopping from one restaurant to another, having only one course in each establishment:

- Drinks
- Appetizer
- Soup
- Salad
- Main course
- Dessert
- After-dinner drinks

For Marrieds Only

73

How many people do you know who have celebrated 288 anniversaries? Well, meet the Claytons, of Nebraska. "We've celebrated our wedding anniversary every month for twenty-four years now. We don't buy gifts every month (we'd be more broke than we are now!), but we do recognize it somehow: with a kiss, a flower, or a short note."

74

Planning to renew your wedding vows in a second ceremony? (You romantic fools, you!) These books may help make the occasion extra special:

- *Weddings for Grownups*, by Carroll Stoner
- *Weddings By Design*, by Richard Leviton

75

Declare it "Wife Appreciation Day"—and act accordingly.

76

Declare him "Husband of the Year"—and treat him like a king for a day.

77

Many couples report fond memories of the time and place that they first met; some of them visit their meeting place yearly; and many of them make a pilgrimage on their tenth, 20th, 25th, 30th, or 40th anniversaries.

Pillowtalk

78

Your bed is a great place to have intimate conversations. Do you give yourselves enough time to lounge, laugh, love, and talk in bed?

79

If you were going to spend an entire Sunday in bed with your lover, what supplies would you need in order to make your bedroom a self-sufficient oasis?

One Day at a Time

80

Give your partner a day. Devote a solid twenty-four hours to him or her.

Take twenty-four slips of paper; number them 1 through 24, and write on each one: "What would you like to do at 6 A.M.?" "What would you like to do at 7 A.M.?" etc.

Wrap your stack of twenty-four hours in an elegant little gift box, along with a new pen (maybe a fancy fountain pen). Your partner will have fun deciding what to do during his or her day—and you'll both have fun living through that special day.

81

Find an "extra" day in the next month and devote that day to your partner. Find or create that extra day by rearranging your schedule; being more efficient at work; delegating some of that work to someone else; limiting your social commitments; paying some neighborhood kids to do your weekend chores.

Tickets

82

Always have at least one set of tickets for an upcoming event tacked to your bulletin board. It's always good to have some special event to look forward to. (The anticipation is half the fun!)

83

"Choice seats on short notice"—great tickets for Broadway shows, sports events, and concerts. Call Tickets On Request at 212-967-5600.

84

It's romantic—but not that unusual—to have tickets to the opera or the Red Sox. Some offbeat romantics have created their own custom "tickets" to the following events and activities:

☞ Dinner for two. (Reserved seating only.)

☞ Season tickets for "Friday Night Mattress Testing."

☞ A personal striptease. (Front row seat guaranteed.)

Outdoor Adventures

85

Camp out in your backyard.

86

Play miniature golf…while dressed in your wedding gown and tuxedo!

87

Your basic picnic.

88

On a summer day…lie on your backs in a field…look for shapes in the clouds…hang out for a couple hours…talk about your hopes and dreams.

89

Rediscover youthful love. Carve your initials in a tree. Inscribe your initials in wet cement on a sidewalk.

90

On a summer night, within a night or two of August 12th every year, you can see dozens of shooting stars every hour! The earth passes through the Perseid Meteor Belt at the same time each year, and we get treated to a show!

91

*G*o parking! (While not officially an "outdoor" activity, we'll let you get away with it.)

91

*G*o on an Outward Bound weekend (or vacation!). Guaranteed to change your perspective on life.

Festivals!

92

*S*treet fairs, county fairs, and state fairs!

93

*C*arnivals and amusement parks!

94

*B*alloon festivals, food festivals, and art festivals!

Dinner for Two

95

*T*ry this next Saturday evening: prepare a five-course dinner—and serve each course in a different room of your home. Choose any rooms you wish, but dessert must be served in the bedroom. Bon appétit!

96

*H*ave a special dinner catered for the two of you at home. No muss, no fuss—just pay for it!

97

*S*end a taxi to pick him up after work; pre-pay the cab fare (including tip!) and instruct the driver to take him to your favorite restaurant, where you'll be waiting for him.

98

*C*reate a meal in which every item of food is fashioned into the shape of a heart.

At-Home Dates

99

Hold a conversation with your lover in the dark. Shut out inputs from your other senses and focus on the sound of your partner's voice: its ups and downs, its unique qualities and quirks. Listen for the love behind the words. Listen. Listen. Listen!

100

Perhaps a hammock would bring the two of you together. Swing lazily between two trees.

101

Create a "Five Senses Evening," during which you and your lover stimulate all five of each other's senses. Enjoy!

102

Do you have a porch? Do you have a porch swing? What more could you ask for?

103

TV dates! If you limit yourself to one or two special shows per week, it can be special, instead of a mind-numbing, time-consuming habit.

104

Plant a garden together. (This will provide you with many built-in dates all summer long.)

105

Play hookey from work. Stay home together. Sleep in late. Make lazy love. Catch a matinee movie.

106

Spend the night composing a love poem together. He writes one verse, she writes the next.

Learning and Loving

107

Spend an afternoon teaching each other to do something you're good at and that your partner wants to learn: cook a special meal; throw a frisbee; change a flat tire; sew a button; play a video game.

108

Start a collection together: stamps, sea shells, wine, beer bottles, baseball cards, old magazines, antique glass, artwork, books, etc.

109

*L*earn a sport together: tennis, scuba diving, sailing, skating, etc.

110

*L*earn a foreign language together.

111

*T*ake music lessons together: violin, piano, guitar.

112

*L*earn to dance. Take classes or use a dance video.

113

*T*ake an adult education class together.

Romance Across the USA

114

Visit all fifty states!

115

Visit every national park across the USA. When you're done with that challenge, start on the state parks!

116

Visit towns with romantic names: Love, Arizona; Romance, Arkansas; Loveland, Colorado; Charm, Ohio; Valentine, Texas; Bliss, New York; Romeo, Michigan; Sweet, Idaho; Joy, Illinois.

Romantic Evenings

117

*R*omantic Evening #1: "An Evening of Romance"

- ᔰ Music: Glenn Miller, George Benson, George Winston, Al Jarreau
- ᔰ Movies: *Casablanca*, *Ghost*, any Fred Astaire movie, *West Side Story*
- ᔰ Food: French bread and cheese
- ᔰ Drink: The most expensive champagne you can afford
- ᔰ Dress: Tuxedos and evening gowns
- ᔰ Props: Candles, red roses, crystal champagne flutes

118

*R*omantic Evening #2: "Beach Party"

- ᔰ Music: Beach Boys, Monkees

- Movies: *Beach Blanket Bingo*
- Food: Grilled burgers, chips
- Drink: Beer
- Dress: Swimming trunks and bikinis
- Props: Cool sunglasses, sand, beach balls, sunscreen

119
*R*omantic Evening #3: "Sex, Sex, Sex!"

- Music: Eurhythmics, *9 ½ Weeks* soundtrack, Sade
- Movies: *9 ½ Weeks*, *Body Heat*, *Emmanuel*
- Food: Smoked oysters, Godiva Chocolates
- Drink: Champagne
- Dress: Optional
- Props: According to your particular liking or fetish!

120

Romantic Evening #4: "1950s Nostalgia"

- Music: Elvis, The Four Freshmen, Buddy Holly
- Movies: Elvis movies, *Picnic*, Doris Day & Rock Hudson movies, *Grease*
- Food: Burgers, onion rings, diner food, Jello
- Drink: Moxie, milk shakes
- Dress: Bobbie sox & saddle shoes, poodle skirts, varsity sweaters
- Props: A '57 Chevy, horn-rimmed glasses

121

Romantic Evening #5: "1960s Nostalgia"

- Music: Beatles, Rolling Stones, Bob Dylan, Janis Joplin
- Movies: *Goldfinger*, *Yellow Submarine*
- Food: Granola
- Drink: Electric Kool-Aid

☞ Dress: Hip-hugger jeans, tie-dyed T-shirts, love beads, head bands

☞ Props: Peace signs, happy face pins, lava lamps, black light posters

Other Romantic Themed Evenings

122

Italian: Italian opera; Italian wine; Italian movie, like *La Dolce Vita*.

High school reunion:

☞ Music: Top hits from when you were a teenager

☞ Movies: Some of your drive-in favorites

☞ Food: The junk food of your adolescence

☞ Drink: Coca-Cola

☞ Dress: Whatever you wore in high school

☞ Props: Stuff from that old, musty chest in your attic

Mall Dates

123

Head for the nearest mall. Enter the record store. Buy everything ever recorded by Al Jarreau and Luther Vandross. And George Winston. Oh, and George Benson. And don't forget William Ackerman. And, as long as you're there, grab everything by David Lanz, too.

124

Many malls host free concerts, antique shows, and other activities.

125

Window-shop and dream together.

126

Create dates centered on specific stores:

🔥 The lingerie shop date: Shop for sexy stuff. Go into the dressing room together. Buy an outfit or two. Model them at home. Enjoy!

🔥 The bookstore date: Browse for books together. Each of you buys two books for the other: one book that you want your partner to read, and one that you know he or she will appreciate. Spend the rest of the evening reading together.

🔥 The bath shop date: Go shopping for soaps, bubblebath powders, massage oils, etc. Then spend the rest of the evening luxuriating in the tub together.

Wild and Crazy

127

The theatrically-oriented among you—or the just plain hams—may want to follow one couple's lead and act out a scene from a favorite movie or play.

This requires both partners to be playful, creative, and flexible. Couples have played Romeo and Juliet; Harry and Sally (from the movie *When Harry Met Sally*); and Rick and Ilsa in a variety of scenes from *Casablanca*.

128

Howard and Janet B. don't act out movie scenes, but they do sometimes "do crazy things" with costumes at home.

Most of their adventures start with homemade costumes. They rented costumes only once: "My tin-foil creation looked more like a robot from *Dr. Who* than a Knight In Shining Armor, so I broke down and rented a suit of armor from a local theatre company."

129

*T*his idea is for couples who like the outdoors, the unusual, and the chance to hit it rich. It's also for very cheap guys looking for engagement rings. You can actually go prospecting for diamonds at Crater of Diamonds State Park in Murfreesboro, Arkansas.

For just $4.50 a day, you can work a furrowed, thirty-five-acre field with shovels, hoes, screens, sifters, or your bare hands. Although most hunters find only bits of quartz, calcite, jasper, and barite, the mine has yielded tens of thousands of diamonds, with about 20 percent of them gem quality.

In 1990, one visitor found a four-carat diamond! It was later cut into a flawless gem worth $38,000. The park, actually the crater of an extinct volcano, is located about halfway between Texarkana and Hot Springs. For more information call 501-285-3113.

Turning Chores Into Dates

130

If you let your inner child out to play, you can make lots of chores into fun times. Adults make raking leaves into work. Children make piles of leaves and leap into them. You and your partner could do the same!

123

You can even make cleaning the bathroom romantic, if you're clever enough about it! Here's how one couple does it: 1) They clean the bathroom together. 2) They time themselves to see how quickly they can do it. 3) They do it in the nude. As you can imagine, they're always bumping into each other, they're hurrying and laughing and making a scene! (And I'll leave it to you to imagine what happens immediately after their chore is done…)

132

And then there's always nude dusting, nude room painting, nude dish washing. (You get the idea.)

Around Town

133

The library date.

134

The coffee shop date.

135

The outdoor concert date.

136

The walk in the park date.

137

Act like a tourist. Call your local Chamber of Commerce and the Convention & Visitors Bureau and get brochures and schedules for all the attractions in your vicinity. Take a tour. Visit the sights.

138

Visit garage sales, flea markets, and craft fairs.

139

Visit art museums, planetariums, and public gardens.

140

Attend a sporting event. Have hot dogs and beer. Cheer for the home team.

Random Ideas

141

Get up an hour early. Have breakfast together at a local diner.

142

Stay up late for a midnight snack. Slip out together to a local coffee shop.

143

Go fly a kite.

144

Learn to bake bread. Bake a pie. Make heart-shaped cookies.

145

Roll out the red carpet—literally—for your lover! Find a red rug, maybe rent one. Roll it out your front door and down the stairs. Treat him like royalty. Make her your Queen-for-a-Day!

146

Split a banana split. Dance the night away. Go singing in the rain.

Seasonal Romance

147

Summer: beaches, walks, summer solstice, surfing, water skiing, rent a convertible.

148

Autumn: leaf watching, Christmas/holiday shopping, autumnal equinox.

149

Winter: ice skating, winter solstice, snowman, sledding, tobogganing, sleigh ride.

150

*S*pring: plant a garden, vernal equinox, fly a kite.

Getting to Know You

151

*I*f your life together were a book or a movie, what kind would it be? A comedy? A horror? A thriller? A mystery? A tragedy? A romantic comedy? A foreign film? A grade-B movie? An X-rated movie? An Academy Award winner? A treasured classic? Fiction or non-fiction?

What roles are each of you playing? Which roles might you like to try on? Hero? Heroine? Good guy? Bad guy? Martyr? Jester? The strong, silent type? The silently-suffering type? The temptress? The prince? The princess? The Wicked Witch? The breadwinner? The mother? The bumbling idiot? The jokester? The handyman? The lover?

152

Get the book *Illusions*, by Richard Bach. Read pages 101 to 113.

153

Take turns asking each other questions from the book *Intimate Questions*.

Stretch Your Limits

154

Read aloud to each other.

155

Have your astrological charts read by a professional astrologer. Great for an evening together, and great for inspiring conversation about your hopes and dreams, your past and future.

Sexy Dates

156

Spend an evening searching for her G-spot. (You may not find it, but you'll both have fun trying!)

157

Aphrodisiac dates! Experiment with some alleged aphrodisiacs. Couldn't hurt. Might help! Oysters, caviar, nutmeg, saffron, ginger, fenugreek, mushrooms, chocolate!

158

Make an appointment to make love. Hey, sometimes you just gotta schedule these things in! Mark it in her day planner; schedule it in his computer; reserve a time on your wall calendar.

159

Lock the doors, draw the curtains, and send the kids away. Then dine in the nude. Or merely scantily clad. (Don't forget to schedule enough time for "dessert.")

160

Meet after work at a local hotel for drinks. Surprise her by having a room reserved. Spend the night pretending you're having an affair.

Games People Play

161

When's the last time the two of you played Monopoly, chess, Scrabble, or cards together?

162

Do the Sunday crossword puzzle together.

163

Go bowling. Shoot pool. Play croquet.

164

Play tennis, badminton, volleyball, or throw a frisbee around.

Fun, Fun, Fun!

165

Do the country western "thing." Learn to two-step. Learn some country line dances. Dress the part: get some cowboy boots and hats.

166

Create a romantic environment with candles. Place dozens of candles throughout your home: in the dining room, living room, up the stairs, in the bathroom, in the bedroom. If this doesn't inspire an evening of romance, nothing will!

ABCs of Love

167

"*Do* you know your ABCs?" Ask your partner to pick a letter. Then, read the list of corresponding words. He or she has twenty-four hours in which to get a romantic gift or perform a romantic gesture based on any one of the key words.

A is for Attitude, Available, Accept, Ardor, Accolades, Admire, Aphrodisiacs, à La Mode, Anniversary, Ambrosia, Ardent, Athens, Australia

B is for Boudoir, B&B, Buttercups, Beaches, Blue, Books, Bing Cherries, Boston, Balloons, Bicycling, Broadway, Brandy, Bubblebaths, Bahamas

C is for Champagne, Creativity, Candlelight, Candy, Chocolate, Convertibles, *Casablanca*, Cognac, Caviar, Chivalry, Crabtree & Evelyn

D is for Diamonds, Dinner, Daffodils, Dancing, Dating, Dolls, *Dirty Dancing*

E is for Enthusiasm, Energy, Excitement, Emeralds, Earrings, Elvis, Erotic, Exotic, Expensive, Escapes

F is for Flirting, Fantasies, Feminine, Faithful, France, Flowers, Fruits, French Kissing, Foreplay

G is for Garters, Gardenias, Godiva, Getaways, Gifts, Glenn Miller, Gourmet, Greece

H is for Hearts, Humor, Hugs, Hideaways, Horses, Honeymoons, Hawaii, Hershey's Kisses, Hyatt

I is for Intimacy, Intrigue, Italy, Inns, Islands, Ingenuity, Ice Cream, Ice Skating, Interdependent, Imaginative, Invitation, Incense

J is for Jewelry, Java, Jasmine, Jello, Jazz, Journey, Joyful, Jacuzzi

K is for Kissing, Kinky, Kittens, Koala Bears

L is for Love, Lingerie, Laughing, Love Letters, Lilacs, Lace, Leather, Leo Buscaglia, Lobsters, Lovemaking, Limousines, Love Songs, London

M is for Monogamy, Marriage, Masculine, M&M's, Massage, Movies, Mistletoe, Music, Mozart

N is for Negligee, Naughty, Nibble, Nighttime, Nubile, Novelty, Nurture, Nymph, Naples, Nightcap, Nape, Nepal, Necklace

O is for Orgasm, Opera, Orchid, Outrageous, Outdoors

P is for Passion, Perfume, Poppies, Poetry, Persimmons, Paris, Polkas, Panties, Pizza, Photos, Pearls, Picnics, Playfulness, Purple

Q is for Quiet, Quaint, Quality, Queen, Quebec, Question, QE2, Quiche, Quiver

R is for Rendezvous, Roses, Rubies, Red, Reading, Rome, Rituals, Riviera, Restful, Rapture, Rings, Rio, Rainbows

S is for Sex

T is for Talking, Teasing, Tulips, Titillating, Theatre, Togetherness, Tickets, Toasts, Toys, Trains, Trinidad

U is for Umbrellas, Uxorious, Undress, Undulate, Urges, Unexpected, Union, Under the Spreading Chestnut Tree

V is for Violets, Virgins, Vibrators, Venice, Venus, Valentines, Vegetables, Victoria's Secret

W is for Wine, Wisteria, Walking Hand-In-Hand, Weddings

X is for X-Rated, Xerographic, Xylophones, Xmas

Y is for Yachts, Yes, Yellow, Yin & Yang, Young-At-Heart

Z is for Zany, Zanzibar, Zeal, Zings, Zodiac, Zurich

Why Be Romantic?!

168

Why be romantic? Because romance is the expression of love. It's the action step of love. You see, without romance, love is merely a concept, an ideal, a nice idea. Romance is what brings love alive in the world.

169

Why be romantic? So you will enjoy life more. Yes, you. Your partner will benefit too—but one of the secrets of true romantics is that we know that our own lives are more fun, joyful, and passionate when we express our feelings of love.

Motivating Your Partner

170

A major reason why some people aren't romantic is that a lack of romance doesn't affect them. You want him (or her) to be more romantic, but he's satisfied with the status quo…"Well, tough luck—that's your problem!" he says/thinks. The solution? Simple: make it his problem. I've observed that people tend to solve problems that they define as problems that relate personally to themselves.

How do you "make it his problem"? Well, you start by telling him upfront what you want (more romance), and how you want it (circle your favorite items in this book!).

Tell him what action you're going to take if he doesn't meet you halfway. Then select activities that you know will strike home with him: Withhold sex. Stop cooking dinner. Stop helping him with selected chores. Stop being romantic toward him.

He'll either get the message or leave. Either way, you win.

171

Positive reinforcement works—negative reinforcement doesn't. Study after study confirms this, and yet most of us ignore it! Here's the simple rule:

Reward behavior that you want repeated.

That's it! If you want her to be more romantic, lavish attention on her every time she's the least bit considerate or loving. DO NOT punish her for not being romantic: nagging doesn't work! You see, positive reinforcement is sometimes a longer, slower process—but its effects are more long-term.

Negative reinforcement, on the other hand, usually works immediately, but resentment soon builds up, and the effects are not long-term.

Romantic Homework

172

Are you ready for some homework? Each of you titles a page "Things I Want You to Do for Me and With Me." The goal here is to create as long a list as possible—at least twenty-five items long.

The lists can cover anything and everything! Now, trade lists. Talk about them. What's realistic? What's unrealistic? How important are certain items? Now, take back your own list and prioritize the top twenty items. (This may take a while!)

Then, trade lists again. Continue removing items until you each have a list of ten things that you want from your partner, and that your partner is likely to act on.

173

*C*reate four lists: a "Wish List"—for things you want; a "Fantasy List"—for sensual and sexual activities you desire; a "Couple's To-Do List"—for activities/restaurants/movies; and a "Dream List"—for travel and vacations.

174

*T*urn romance into a habit—a good habit. It may feel awkward, unnatural, or contrived at first, but keep at it!

Research has shown that it takes about three weeks to form new habits. If you repeat an activity or thought pattern several times a day over three weeks, you'll get it ingrained into that stubborn brain of yours! Go for it!

For Men Only

175

Many men view romance as "giving in" to a woman. It makes perfect sense to me that you'd resist being romantic if you see it that way.

It's natural for people to resist what they view as coercion. Here's a suggestion: Don't give in. Don't do what she expects. Don't do what society expects. Don't try to live up to some fairy tale of what the perfect man should be. Don't follow some soap opera stereotype of a great guy.

Here's what you could do instead: Express your own feelings in your own way. That's all there is to it. It is possible to retain your individuality, express your own feelings, do it your own way, and please her—all at the same time!

176

Romance is like exercising: you know it's good for you, but it's difficult—sometimes actually painful!—at first.

But, as any coach will tell you, the benefits will keep building if you just keep up the effort. And after a while, this "chore" will become a habit, and you'll be healthier and happier.

A lot of guys who are He-Men in the muscle department, and Supermen in the boardroom, are 90-Pound Weaklings when in comes to intimacy and love. C'mon, guys, don't let the women kick sand in your face!

177

Plan a date for Superbowl Sunday! (After she wakes up from fainting, she'll be delighted!) Tape the game on your VCR so you can watch it later, of course.

For Women Only

178

*P*sst! Ladies! Here's the worst-kept secret in the world: guys do want and need romance. I don't know why we play this game around it, but most men do.

Frankly, many men are quite sentimental. And every tough guy has a soft spot. Look for it—you'll find it.

179

*H*ard to motivate your guy? Is he a sports nut? Great! Do something he'll understand: Put him on a "Point System"—turn romance into a "game."

Write your own rules, post them on the refrigerator door, create score sheets, and keep statistics. Award him points for various romantic activities.

When he racks up one hundred points, he wins something that truly motivates him. You decide what: anything from sex to pizza, or from backrubs to doing his most hated chore for him!

180

Some inspiration for "erotic dates" can be found in the pages of various masterpieces of "erotica for women":

↬ *Slow Hand: Women Writing Erotica*, edited by Michele Slung

↬ *Women On Top*, by Nancy Friday

↬ *The Second Gates of Paradise*, by Alberto Manguel

↬ *Erotica*, edited by Margaret Reynolds

Extra Items

181

One way to generate romantic ideas is to "break the pattern" of your daily lives. Changing any one thing, or a combination of them, has the potential for creating new and exciting opportunities in your lives.

What are your patterns? What time do you wake up in the morning? What do you eat for breakfast? Where do you eat? How do you dress? How long do you work? Where do you drive? What do you do with the kids? What do you watch on TV? How often do you talk by phone with each other?

Erotic Dates

182

What kind of fun could you have with Chocolate Body Paints?! A handy set of "His & Hers" 8 oz. jars are available from The Celebration Fantastic Catalog. Call 800-CELEBRATE.

183

Forget "strip poker"—try playing "strip dinner!" With each course, you each remove one article of clothing! Make sure you plan plenty of courses!

Mood Music

184

For creating a mellow mood, albums by Nicholas Gunn:

- The Sacred Fire
- The Music of the Grand Canyon

185

For creating an erotic mood, two albums by Enigma:

- MCMXC A.D.
- The Cross of Change

186

For creating a thoughtful mood, albums by George Winston:

- Summer

- Autumn

- Winter Into Spring

187

Music for creating an uplifting mood, by Eric Tingstad and Nancy Rumbel:

- Homeland

- Give and Take

- In the Garden

188

*M*usic for creating a mystical mood, by Andreas Vollenweider:

❧ *White Winds*

❧ *Down to the Moon*

189

*T*he world's most romantic piano concertos (take my word for it):

❧ Mozart's Piano Concerto No. 21 in C

❧ Beethoven's Piano Concerto No. 5 in E-flat

❧ Schumann's Concerto in A Minor for Piano and Orchestra

❧ Grieg's Concerto in A Minor for Piano and Orchestra

Fun, Fun, Fun!

190

This one could keep the two of you busy for weeks! Have a custom jigsaw puzzle created for the two of you, based on your design, artwork, or photo.

191

What's your favorite card game? Spend an evening playing poker or gin rummy, kings or cribbage. Place some bets to make it more interesting.

192

Play strip poker together! For the more intellectual among you, play strip chess!

193

Be conventional—attend a convention together. Fanatics love to gather! Science fiction fanatics, Star Trekkers, comic book collectors, quilt makers, car buffs, RVers, Beatles fans, guys named Bob, romance novel writers, etc.

Kinda Crazy

194

Serenade her! Sing her favorite love song, or "Your Song," to her. Get a friend to accompany you on guitar.

195

If your partner is a beer lover to rival Norm Peterson…plan a date to "Beer Camp!" Believe it or not, The American Museum of Brewing History and

Arts, in Fort Mitchell, Kentucky, runs a three-day Beer Camp!
Call 800-323-4917.

186

For creating a romantic atmosphere everywhere you go, keep candles in your car at all times. Bring them into McDonald's when you stop for a burger! (Why should you care if other people think you're strange?!)

187

Kidnap him! Blindfold him; drive him around town until he's thoroughly lost; then reveal your destination: his favorite restaurant, the ballpark, or maybe a romantic inn.

Use Your Creativity

198

Romantic Challenge #1: Create a date that is classic and conservative but thoughtful to the extreme.

199

Romantic Challenge #2: Create a date that is sexy to the point of nearly being illegal.

200

Romantic Challenge #3: Create a date that is not necessarily wild but is totally unexpected from a person of your personality style.

Going Places!

201

*F*eeling adventurous? Pack two bags, call your travel agent, and ask for discount tickets for vacation packages leaving anytime in the next twenty-four hours. Regardless of what the destination is—go!

202

*I*s your honey a *Wizard of Oz* fanatic? If so, take him or her to the Judy Garland Museum! Rare photos, rare recordings, and memorabilia. The Yellow Brick Road is in Grand Rapids, Minnesota. Call 218-327-9276.

203

*T*ry an "ultra all-inclusive luxury resort for couples only" at one of Sandals Resorts on Jamaica, Antigua, St. Lucia, or Barbados. Call 888-SANDALS.

204

*I*f money is no object, you may want to take your honey on a three-week, round-the-world trip on the Concorde! Only $52,000 per person! Call INTRAV at 800-456-8100.

205

*V*isit the real bridges of Madison County—in Winterset, Iowa!

Togetherness

206

*B*ake Christmas cookies together. Let your creativity run wild while decorating them.

207

𝒟esign your own holiday cards. You don't have to be Picasso to be creative!

208

𝒟esign a whole line of greeting cards from the two of you. Create a distinctive style that all your friends and family will recognize as they receive custom birthday cards, anniversary cards, holiday cards, Halloween cards, etc., from the two of you.

Poetic Dates

209

ℋe plays Romeo, she plays Juliet. Read aloud to each other.

210

Pick a passage from your "Favorite Book of All Time." Read it aloud to your partner. Share with him or her its significance in your life.

211

Pick a steamy passage from an erotic book to read aloud to each other in bed. Some modest suggestions:

- *Little Birds*, by Anaïs Nin
- *Lady Chatterley's Lover*, by D.H. Lawrence
- *Tropic of Cancer*, by Henry Miller
- *Yellow Silk*, edited by Lily Pond and Richard Russo

212

*F*ind a copy of Elizabeth Barrett Browning's poem "How do I love thee? Let me count the ways." Spend an evening rewriting the poem to list the many ways you love each other.

Rendezvous

213

*M*eet for drinks after work.

214

*M*eet for lunch during a busy week.

215

Meet at a local motel for a little "afternoon delight."

216

Meet for dinner at the airport. Dream about faraway places.

217

Meet at work for an in-office picnic.

Up, Up and Away!

218

Go for a romantic ride in a hot air balloon.

219

Have you ever considered taking flying lessons together?

220

For the slightly courageous, try bungee jumping!

221

For the extremely courageous, try hang gliding!

222

For the truly courageous, try sky diving!

Out and About

223

*B*efore you can sail off into the sunset together, it might be helpful to take sailing lessons together.

224

*T*hey tell me that surfing is a blast.

225

*H*ow about scuba diving?

226

*H*ow about an afternoon of snorkeling?

227

How about a day of just sitting on the beach, reading, talking, and sipping daiquiris?

228

While on the beach, challenge each other to a sandcastle building contest. The loser has to run to the ice cream stand for snacks.

Role Playing

229

While out to dinner, take on the roles of characters from your favorite movie. How would Indiana Jones be enjoying dinner? What would Princess Leia talk about this evening?

230

Spend an evening out pretending that you're characters from your favorite movie, TV show, or book. James Bond? Scarlett O'Hara? Captain James T. Kirk? Lucille Ball?

231

Each of you choose a favorite character from the movies, Broadway, or literature, and act out meeting one another, falling in love, and seducing one another. (Could be fun for an evening—could go on for weeks!)

232

Pretend you're tourists visiting your own town. Visit places you've never gotten around to before. See things through new eyes.

233

*P*retend you're vacationing foreigners who don't speak any English. Have fun asking directions and ordering in restaurants while pretending to not understand English.

Party On!

234

*T*hrow a surprise birthday party for your partner.

235

*T*hrow a surprise party for no specific reason.

236

Guys: Get together with several of your buddies and throw a surprise "Wife/Girlfriend Appreciation Party." The highlight of the party is when you toast the gals with champagne: each of you, one at a time, stands up and recites a romantic, prewritten toast to your honey.

237

Gals: Get together with some of your girlfriends and plan a surprise "Husband/Boyfriend Appreciation Party." Serve their favorite beer; maybe watch a football game on TV; maybe get together and write a song about all of them—then sing it to them!

238

Host a wine tasting party.

239

Host a "Taste Test" party, in which you hold blind taste testings to see of your friends can identify these foods:

ॐ Coke vs. Pepsi vs. Diet Coke vs. Diet Pepsi, etc.

ॐ Budweiser vs. Heineken vs. Coors vs. Miller, etc.

ॐ Different peanut butter brands

ॐ Different potato chip brands

ॐ Different types of breakfast cereal

Acting Up

240

Hire a limousine for the evening. Make reservations at the best restaurant in town. Dress in a tuxedo and an evening gown. Hire a photographer to snap

your picture as you arrive at the restaurant. Pretend you're famous—watch people gawk and try to figure out who you are!

241

Join a local community theatre group. Whether you're playing the lead, singing in the chorus, or designing scenery, you'll have a blast!

242

Act out your favorite erotic fantasy together.

243

Choose fantasy roles—and stay in character for an entire day!

Calming Down

244

Learn to meditate together. Buy a book or take a class together to get you started.

245

Take a weekend to calm down…attend a religious, spiritual, or meditational retreat.

246

Take a different kind of vacation…one designed to deepen your spirit and expand your mind. Check out a great book called *Vacations That Can Change Your Life: Adventures, Retreats & Workshops for the Mind, Body & Spirit*, by Ellen Lederman.

247

Make a cassette tape of romantic, instrumental music. Go for a drive in the country while listening to the soothing sounds. Don't speak a word.

Getting Out

248

Run a race together. Maybe a local "Fun Run." Maybe a fundraiser for a local charity.

249

Get serious about it: run some 10K races.

250

*G*et really serious about it: train to run a marathon.

251

*G*rab your backpacks and go for a day hike.

Marathons

252

*C*atch a movie marathon at a local theatre.

253

*C*reate your own movie marathon by renting a bunch of movies that form a theme.

254

Create a TV show marathon. Videotape a bunch of your favorite TV shows over several months. Save them up for a twenty-four hour TV marathon.

255

Spend a night of non-stop, marathon lovemaking!

Picture This

256

Buy a bunch of cheap, throw-away cameras. Spend a Saturday afternoon on a "Photo Safari."

257

Buy an expensive camera, take photography classes together, and get serious about it.

258

Take turns shooting portrait shots of each other. Try to capture the true essence of each other's personality.

259

For the truly adventurous, spend an evening posing for elegant, erotic photos of each other.

Group Activities

260

Join a local Marriage Encounter group. You'll deepen your relationship with like-minded couples.

261

Join a local political campaign.

262

Take horseback riding lessons together.

263

Play Twister with a group of friends.

Something Old

264

Attend a program sponsored by your local historical society.

265

Spend the day with your oldest living relative. Share stories about your family history.

266

Go on a tour of old homes in your area.

267

Grab your high school yearbooks and spend an evening sharing memories.

Something New

268

Learn to play a video game. (You may need to hire a local youngster to teach you.)

269

Whether or not you're interested in buying a new house, attend some local Open Houses. Discuss your ideas of the "Perfect Home."

270

Visit new restaurants in your area. Don't go to the same old places on every date!

271

Catch a new act at a local comedy club.

Friends

272

Gather a group of friends and plan "Progressive Dinners" once a month.

273

Gather a group of friends, all of whom have small children, and take turns hosting "Group Pajama Parties." You take turns hosting all the kids overnight, so all the other couples can have more time alone.

274

Throw a massive Superbowl party. Attendees must dress as football players, cheerleaders, referees, or crazy fans!

275

Host a "Murder Mystery" party. Who-done-it?!

Roll the Dice

276

Head to Las Vegas for the weekend. (Or to Atlantic City!)

277

Gamble on a Mississippi River Boat!

278

*P*lay a complete, non-stop game of Monopoly.

279

*L*ist twelve different sexual activities on a sheet of paper. Roll two dice to determine which activity the two of you will share tonight! (She rolls the dice this time—he rolls the dice the next time.) Nobody loses!

Questions and Answers

280

*D*o you celebrate one another at any time other than your anniversary? Celebrate your anniversary every month.

281

*H*ow did you meet? Where did you meet? Visit that place. Reenact your meeting. Take some artistic license to make your "second meeting" memorably romantic!

282

*D*o you rush through meals, or do you savor them together? Make time. Create your own personal rituals around meals.

283

*W*hen's the last time you watched a sunset together? A sunrise? All it takes is a little desire, a little time, and a little planning.

Asking for a Date

284

Send him an email invitation to a date.

285

Attach a note to a single red rose. The note includes one line from a romantic song, along with your request for a date.

286

Buy two tickets to something (a show, a sporting event, a concert) and mail them to your partner, along with a note asking him or her for a date.

287

Fax your request for a date! (Make sure it doesn't get intercepted by an office colleague!)

288

Write a short poem that describes the date you're proposing.

Theme Dates

289

Romantic Evening #1: "Erotic Romance"

Set a sexy mood with music by Sade or Enigma; light the scene with candles; serve champagne and a tray of aphrodisiacs; dress in your sexiest outfit; remove all distractions; draw the curtains…and prepare to spend an entire evening in sexual exploration.

290

Romantic Evening #2: "1950s Nostalgia"

Spin those old 45s by Elvis, The Four Freshmen, and Buddy Holly. Dress in bobbie socks, saddle shoes, a poodle skirt, or a varsity sweater. Serve burgers and moxie. And take your honey for a romantic ride in a '57 Chevy!

291

Romantic Evening #3: "1960s Nostalgia"

Dress in hip-hugger jeans, tie-dyed T-shirts, love beads, and head bands. Blast music by the Beatles, Rolling Stones, Bob Dylan, and Janis Joplin. Make love by the light of your lava lamp.

292

Romantic Evening #4: "High School Nostalgia"

Gather music from when you were a teenager; rent some movies that were big during those years; dig out your high school year books...and create a custom date based on your own history.

293
Romantic Evening #5: "Viva Italiana!"
Gather all things Italian: Wines, foods, opera, posters, and movies. Create an evening of romance based on those hot-blooded Mediterraneans!

More Romantic Evenings

294
Some modest suggestions to spark your imagination:

Romantic Evening #6: "New York, New York"

Romantic Evening #7: "Lingerie Fashion Show"

Romantic Evening #8: "Gourmet Delight"

Romantic Evening #9: "The Bridges of Madison County"

You Can Quote Me On That!

295

Create a romantic date based on the following quote:

> "I do love nothing in the world so well as you; is not that strange?"
>
> ~ William Shakespeare

Copy this quote onto a card, give it to your partner, and plan to do something really strange. (Defining exactly what constitutes "strange" is up to you!)

296

Create a date based on this romantic quote:

> "My most brilliant achievement was my ability to be able to persuade my wife to marry me."
>
> ~ Winston Churchill

Plan a date—an outrageous, stupendously wonderful date—that will become your most brilliant achievement.

297

Create a romantic date based on this quote:

"Love is, above all, the gift of oneself."

~ Jean Anouilh

Copy this quote onto a card, give it to your partner, and create a date in which you give yourself to your partner.

298

Create a romantic date based on this quote:

"A love song is just a caress set to music."

~ Sigmund Romberg

Copy this quote onto a card, give it to your partner, and spend an evening combining the two concepts of love songs and caresses!

299

Create a romantic date based on this quote:

> *"The heart that loves is always young."*
>
> ~ Greek proverb

Copy this quote onto a card, give it to your partner, and do something that proves you're still young: go to a playground; go on a picnic; go for a stroll.

300

Create a date based on this romantic quote:

> *"The madness of love is the greatest of heaven's blessings."*
>
> ~ Plato

Copy this quote onto a card, give it to your partner, and plan something "mad," like taking a surprise day off of work.

301

Create a date based on an inspirational quote:

"God is love, and love is joy. All the universe has come from love and unto love all things return."

~ Juan Mascaro

Copy this quote onto a card, give it to your partner, and plan a joyful date that reconnects you with your spiritual beliefs.

302

Create a date based on this quote:

"Love, you know, seeks to make happy rather than to be happy."

~ Ralph Connor

Copy this quote onto a card, give it to your partner, and plan a date that is specifically designed to touch his or her heart.

303

Create a date based on a quote:

> *"Love is a little haven of refuge from the world."*
>
> ~ Bertrand Russell

Copy this quote onto a card, give it to your partner, and create your very own haven of refuge in your home. Maybe you'll have to escape to a bed and breakfast in order to find a safe haven.

304

Create a date based on a quote: be on the look-out for quotes that can inspire date ideas. You're surrounded by great quotes all the time—in newspapers, magazines, books, TV, and radio.

Song-Inspired Dates

305

Create a date based on the song:

> "Eight Days a Week"
> by The Beatles

Give your partner a copy of this song, and find a way to squeeze an "extra" day out of a week sometime next month.

306

Create a date based on the song:

> "Chattanooga Choo-Choo"
> by Glenn Miller

Give your partner a copy of this song, and get two tickets for a train ride—maybe a dinner train.

308

Create a date based on the song:

>"Light My Fire"
>by The Doors

Give your partner a copy of this song, build a fire in the fireplace and light your lover's fire!

309

Create a date based on a song:

>"You Are the Sunshine of My Life"
>by Stevie Wonder

Give your partner a copy of this song, and spend a day out in the sun! Hit a beach, dine outdoors, drive a convertible!

Book a Date!

309

Create a date based on the book:

Love Signs
by Linda Goodman

Give your partner a copy of this book; it details the pros and cons of every match-up of two Zodiac signs. Spend an evening analyzing your relationship!

310

Create a date based on the book:

The Joy of Sex
by Alex Comfort

Give your partner a copy of this book. Pick a page. Follow the recipe!

311

Create a date based on the book:

> *Off the Beaten Path—A Guide to More Than 1,000 Scenic and*
> *Interesting Places Still Uncrowded and Inviting*

Give your partner a copy of this book. Find someplace nearby and head there ASAP.

312

Create a date based on the book:

> *The Art of Kissing*
> by William Cane

Give your partner a copy of this book. Spend an evening exploring different kissing techniques!

313

Create a date based on the book:

A Whack on the Side of the Head: How You Can Be More Creative
by Roger vonOech

Get a copy of this book, and spend an evening brainstorming ideas for dates with your partner.

Movie-Inspired Dates

314

Create a date based on the movie:

Dirty Dancing

Watch the movie together, then create your own, custom "Dirty Dance"…and dance your way into bed!

315

Create a date based on the movie:

Love Story

Watch the movie together. Discuss what the two of you would do if one of you had only weeks to live. What would you change about your lives in order to cherish each other more?!

316

Create a date based on the movie:

Somewhere in Time

Watch the movie together. Imagine the two of you meeting in a different era. Talk about your favorite time period. Rent costumes from that time—fantasize!

317

Create a date based on the movie:

From Here to Eternity

Watch the movie together. Head for the nearest beach…you'll know what to do!

Mission Impossible

318

Do the impossible: Get him Superbowl tickets!

319

Do the impossible: Meet her at the airport when she knows you're tied-up and can't make it. Devote the entire evening to her.

320

Do the impossible: Get tickets to a sold-out show.

Full of Hot Air!

321

Visit one of America's many hot air balloon festivals:

- ⌇ The U.S. National Hot Air Balloon Festival: early August, in Indianola, Iowa. Call 515-961-8415.

- ⌇ The New York State Festival of Balloons: late August/early September, in Dansville, New York. Call 716-335-8885.

- ⌇ The International Balloon Fiesta: mid-October, in Albuquerque, New Mexico. Call 888-422-7277

Romantic Classics

322

Dinner at a fine French restaurant. Propose a toast to one another with every glass of wine.

323

Visit the place where you first met; where you went on your first date; where you had your first kiss. Relive the moment.

Also by Gregory J.P. Godek:

1001 Ways To Be Romantic
5th Anniversary Edition of the Bestselling Classic!

10,000 Ways to Say I Love You

Intimate Questions

LoveQuotes Coupons

I Love You Coupons

To order these books or any other of our many publications, please contact your local bookseller, gift store, or call Sourcebooks, Inc. Books by Gregory J.P. Godek are available in book and gift stores across North America. Get a copy of our catalog by writing or faxing:

Sourcebooks, Inc.
P. O. Box 4410
Naperville, IL 60567-4410
(630) 961-3900
FAX: (630) 961-2168